TUNA
SEA CHICKEN
1386

For Hazel and Gene and all your adventures at the zoo—Kate and Jol

For Niharika, Shay, Zola and Mica—Ronojoy

Scholastic Press
An imprint of Scholastic Australia Pty Limited (ABN 11 000 614 577)
PO Box 579 Gosford NSW 2250
www.scholastic.com.au

Part of the Scholastic Group
Sydney • Auckland • New York • Toronto • London • Mexico City
New Delhi • Hong Kong • Buenos Aires • Puerto Rico

Published by Scholastic Australia in 2024.

ISBN: 978-1-76129-451-8 (hardback)

A catalogue record for this book is available from the National Library of Australia

Typeset in Olliefat.

Ronojoy Ghosh created these illustrations digitally.

Printed in China by RR Donnelley.
Scholastic Australia's policy, in association with RR Donnelley, is to use papers that are renewable and made efficiently from wood grown in responsibly managed forests, so as to minimise its environmental footprint.

10 9 8 7 6 5 4 24 25 26 27 28 / 2

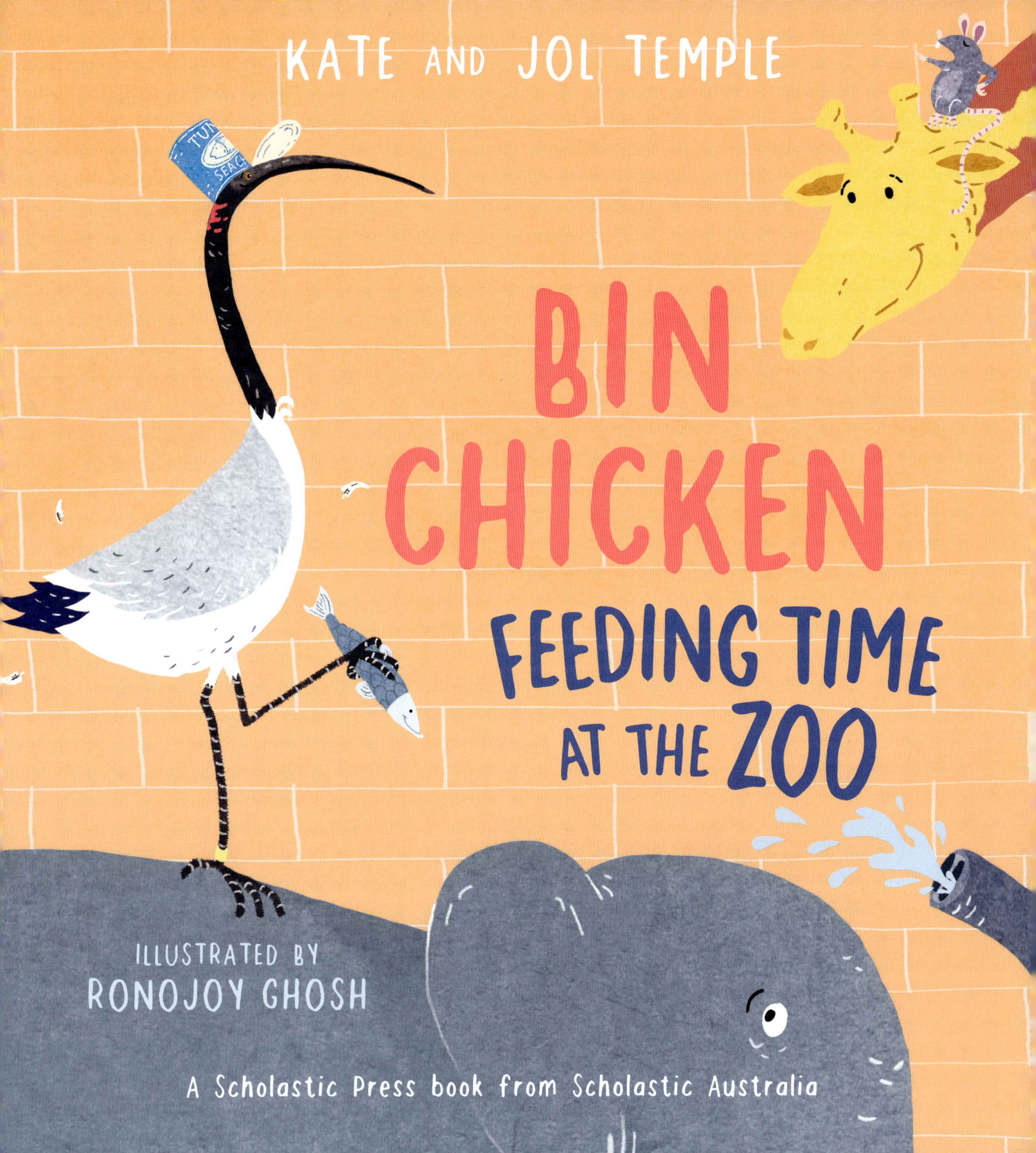
KATE AND JOL TEMPLE
BIN CHICKEN
FEEDING TIME AT THE ZOO
ILLUSTRATED BY
RONOJOY GHOSH
A Scholastic Press book from Scholastic Australia

By a grand fountain, near a park bench,

stands a fabulous ibis that lets out a stench.

She's been wading through bin juice and sticky grime,
and her tummy is rumbling . . . it's nearly **lunchtime!**

'Where shall I feast?' she wonders out loud,
and looks up to see a big, bustling crowd.

Lines of children on a school outing.

Flustered teachers

counting heads,

shouting,

'Stick together,
you lot!
Stay in the queue!'

But the kids are excited

because they're at the **ZOO**.

Ibis struts past them

to the first enclosure she sees,

where a blotchy **giraffe** pokes its head

through the trees.

'What's on the menu?' Ibis honks from the eaves.

Ibis flies off, shrubs don't sound delicious.

Maybe the elephant will be more ambitious?

She lands on something huge and grey.

'Where's the **elephant?**' she begins to say.

'You're **standing on me!'** says the big hunk.

Ibis jumps back, avoiding its trunk.

'I've got some bad news,' it says with a huff.

'I love to eat **straw** even though I look tough.'

With that, a bale of hay is tossed over the wall,

so Ibis takes off to follow a strange barking call . . .

Ibis lands close to a sparkling blue pool,
near a bucket of fish that
would make a bird **drool!**

She struts over to gobble sardines in brine
when a keeper appears and points at a sign.

'This isn't your lunch. It's just not for you.
We don't feed **bin chickens** here at the zoo.'

'**How rude!**' says Ibis. 'What a nerve!
I guess that means this place is **self-serve!**'
Ibis snaps at a fish and takes off in a flash . . .
what happens next makes quite a **splash!**

A slippery seal leaps after that runaway snack,
with a **flip** and a **flick**, it snatches it back!

TUNA
SEA CHICKEN

Ibis loses her balance, the fish is a loss!

And she slaps right into a **HUGE fairy floss!**

Startled to be in this sugary cloud,

Ibis makes for the sky and flies over the crowd.

Honk!

Over the zebra paddock and lion enclosure,

our puffy pink Ibis is in need of composure.

Despite her strange outfit, she just keeps on flapping,

and that's when she hears **cheering** and **clapping**.

Ibis widens her wings and begins to slow . . .

BIRD SHOW

. . . and performs a crash-landing at the **bird show!**

Buzzards, owls, brolgas, even a hawk.

Parrots, kookaburras, cockatoos that talk!

The keeper throws delicious **treats** into the air,

and the clever birds catch them without a care.

'Nice catch!' honks Ibis.

'You're just like **me!**'

'Absolutely,' says Owl from a nearby tree.

Some of us swoop or dive like a plover.
And others just nibble the things we discover.
TUNA
SEA CHICKEN
CLANCY

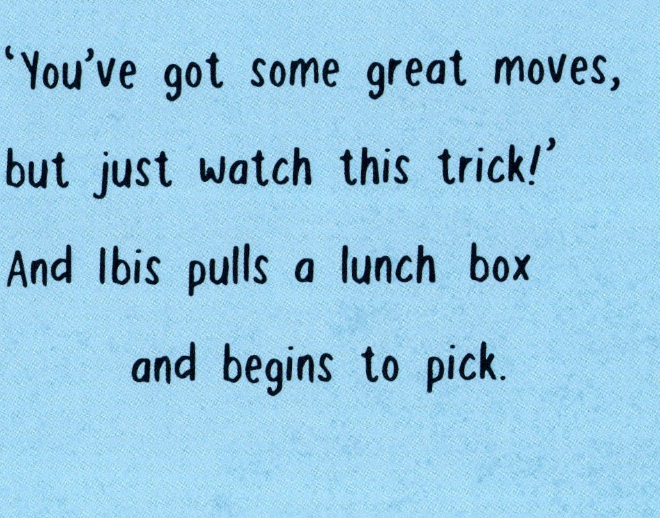

'You've got some great moves,
but just watch this trick!'
And Ibis pulls a lunch box
and begins to pick.

With a click and a clack
she's opened that box.

'No!' yells the teacher.
'That bird's a sly fox!'

The zookeeper pounces, the teachers rush round,

but in all the fuss, **food** hits the ground.

Hot chips, crackers, an **ice-cream** melts in the sun.

Cut-up apple, cheese cubes and

half a **sticky bun!**

Ibis wastes no time—

Gobble! Slurp! Crunch!

She digs into the feast and honks,

'Thanks for lunch!'

After a delicious dessert of old apple cores,

Ibis takes to the stage

for a round of **applause**.

A
1-24
A
B
C
D
E
F
G

I LOVE THESE EARRINGS!